A SCRIPTURAL ROSARY FOR
JUSTICE AND PEACE

Includes the Luminous Mysteries

Catholic Campaign for Human Development
United States Conference of Catholic Bishops

Washington, DC

Introduction

From the Church's earliest days, those seeking to be faithful followers of Jesus Christ have looked to Mary for example, strength, and encouragement. As the first disciple, the first one to say "yes" to all that it means to welcome the presence of Jesus Christ into one's own life, she is a model for us to follow. Like Mary, we are invited to listen to Jesus attentively and to change the shape of our lives in order to allow his work to be done here in our own life and times. Like Mary, we are invited to believe in him, to follow him, and to seek the light of his presence in seasons of sorrow as well as joy.

This resource, *A Scriptural Rosary for Justice and Peace,* has been prepared by the Catholic Campaign for Human Development of the United States Conference of Catholic Bishops in order to help those praying the rosary to call upon our Blessed Mother with both a spirit of humility and a commitment to justice. This revised edition includes the new Luminous Mysteries, suggested by Pope John Paul II to allow prayerful reflection on the life and ministry of Jesus. Praying these mysteries provides us with new opportunities to see Jesus more fully, as Mary does, and then to find him in the faces of those who still struggle to live with dignity.

In praying the rosary, we open ourselves to the mystery of God's love by focusing our attention on the Scriptures—God's Word, which continues to speak to us today. The rhythm of these prayers that have formed, challenged, and comforted Christians worldwide for many centuries enrolls us in what John Paul II calls "the school of Mary." Our Holy Father reminds us that our focus on the life of Jesus "cannot fail to draw attention to the face of Christ in others, especially in the most afflicted."[1]

Hail Holy Queen, Mother of mercy, our life, our sweetness, and our hope. Show us the blessed fruit of thy womb, Jesus. Pray for us, O Holy Mother of God, that we may be made worthy of the promises of Christ.

Robert J. Vitillo

Rev. Robert J. Vitillo
Executive Director
Catholic Campaign for Human Development
United States Conference of Catholic Bishops

---

1 John Paul II, Apostolic Letter *On the Most Holy Rosary* (*Rosarium Virginis Mariae*) (October 16, 2002) (Washington, DC: United States Conference of Catholic Bishops—Libreria Editrice Vaticana, 2002), no. 40.

Prayers

Our Father
>Our Father, who art in heaven,
>Hallowed be thy name;
>Thy kingdom come;
>Thy will be done on earth as it is in heaven.
>Give us this day our daily bread;
>And forgive us our trespasses
>As we forgive those who trespass against us;
>And lead us not into temptation,
>But deliver us from evil.
>Amen.

Hail Mary
>Hail Mary, full of grace,
>The Lord is with thee!
>Blessed art thou among women,
>And blessed is the fruit of thy womb, Jesus.
>Holy Mary, mother of God,
>Pray for us sinners,
>Now and at the hour of our death.
>Amen.

Glory Be
>Glory be to the Father, and to the Son,
>   and to the Holy Spirit;
>as it was in the beginning, is now,
>   and will be for ever.
>Amen.

First Joyful Mystery
THE ANNUNCIATION

The angel Gabriel announces to Mary that she is to become the mother of the Messiah.
Our Father . . .

In the sixth month, the angel Gabriel was sent from God to a town of Galilee called Nazareth, to a virgin betrothed to a man named Joseph, of the house of David, and the virgin's name was Mary. *Lk 1:26-27*
Hail Mary . . .

Hail, favored one! The Lord is with you. *Lk 1:28*
Hail Mary . . .

Do not be afraid, Mary, for you have found favor with God. Behold, you will conceive in your womb and bear a son, and you shall name him Jesus. *Lk 1:30-31*
Hail Mary . . .

He will be great and will be called Son of the Most High, and the Lord God will give him the throne of David his father. *Lk 1:32*
Hail Mary . . .

I, the LORD, am your God, who brought you out of the land of Egypt, that place of slavery. You shall not have other gods besides me. *Ex 20:2-3*
Hail Mary . . .

Learn to do good. / Make justice your aim: redress the wronged. *Is 1:17*
Hail Mary . . .

Hear the orphan's plea, defend the widow. *Is 1:17*
Hail Mary . . .

The LORD does righteous deeds, / brings justice to all the oppressed. *Ps 103:6*
Hail Mary . . .

Justice will bring about peace; / right will produce calm and security. *Is 32:17*
Hail Mary . . .

For nothing will be impossible for God. *Lk 1:37*
Hail Mary . . .
Glory be . . .

LORD JESUS, TEACH US TO FOLLOW
IN YOUR WAY OF HUMILITY.

Second Joyful Mystery
THE VISITATION

*Mary visits her cousin Elizabeth to share the
Good News.*
Our Father . . .

Most blessed are you among women, and blessed is
the fruit of your womb. *Lk 1:42*
Hail Mary . . .

My soul proclaims the greatness of the Lord; my spirit
rejoices in God my savior. *Lk 1:46-47*
Hail Mary . . .

For he has looked upon his handmaid's lowliness; behold,
from now on will all ages call me blessed. *Lk 1:48*
Hail Mary . . .

He has shown might with his arm, dispersed the arro-
gant of mind and heart. *Lk 1:51*
Hail Mary . . .

The hungry he has filled with good things; the rich he
has sent away empty. *Lk 1:53*
Hail Mary . . .

I rejoice heartily in the LORD, / in my God is the joy of my soul; / For he has clothed me with a robe of salvation, / and wrapped me in a mantle of justice. *Is 61:10*
Hail Mary . . .

The LORD raises the needy from the dust, / lifts the poor from the ash heap. *Ps 113:7*
Hail Mary . . .

The LORD is on high, but cares for the lowly / and knows the proud from afar. *Ps 138:6*
Hail Mary . . .

When the just cry out, the LORD hears / and rescues them from all distress. *Ps 34:18*
Hail Mary . . .

I will bless the LORD at all times; / praise shall be always in my mouth. / My soul will glory in the LORD / that the poor may hear and be glad. *Ps 34:1-2*
Hail Mary . . .
Glory be . . .

LORD JESUS, FILL OUR HEARTS WITH
YOUR LOVE OF JUSTICE.

Third Joyful Mystery
THE NATIVITY

The Savior of the world is born in a manger.
Our Father . . .

Joseph too went up from Galilee from the town of
Nazareth to Judea, to the city of David that is called
Bethlehem, because he was of the house and family of
David, to be enrolled with Mary, his betrothed, who
was with child. *Lk 2:4-5*
Hail Mary . . .

The time came for her to have her child, and she gave
birth to her firstborn son. *Lk 2:6-7*
Hail Mary . . .

She wrapped him in swaddling clothes and laid him in
a manger, because there was no room for them in the
inn. *Lk 2:7*
Hail Mary . . .

I proclaim to you goodnews of great joy that will be
for all the people. For today in the city of David a
savior has been born for you who is Messiah and Lord.
Lk 2:10-11
Hail Mary . . .

So they went in haste and found Mary and Joseph,
and the infant lying in the manger. When they saw
this, they made known the message that had been

told. . . . *Lk 2:16-17*
Hail Mary . . .

When Herod realized that he had been deceived by the magi, he became furious. He ordered the massacre of all the boys in Bethlehem . . . two years old and under. *Mt 2:16*
Hail Mary . . .

The angel of the Lord appeared to Joseph in a dream and said, "Rise, take the child and his mother, flee to Egypt, and stay there until I tell you." *Mt 2:13*
Hail Mary . . .

When Herod had died, behold, the angel of the Lord appeared in a dream to Joseph in Egypt and said, "Rise, take the child and his mother and go to the land of Israel." *Mt 2:19-20*
Hail Mary . . .

But when he heard that Archelaus was ruling over Judea in place of his father Herod, he was afraid to go back there. *Mt 2:22*
Hail Mary . . .

And Mary kept all these things, reflecting on them in her heart. *Lk 2:19*
Hail Mary . . .
Glory be . . .

LORD JESUS, TEACH US TO LIVE AS
YOU DID: FULLY, WITH JOY.

Fourth Joyful Mystery
THE PRESENTATION

Mary and Joseph take Jesus to the temple in Jerusalem to present him to the Lord.
Our Father . . .

Now there was a man in Jerusalem whose name was Simeon. This man was righteous and devout, awaiting the consolation of Israel, and the holy Spirit was upon him. *Lk 2:25*
Hail Mary . . .

It had been revealed to him by the holy Spirit that he should not see death before he had seen the Messiah of the Lord. *Lk 2:26*
Hail Mary . . .

When the parents brought in the child Jesus to perform the custom of the law in regard to him, he took him into his arms and blessed God. *Lk 2:27-28*
Hail Mary . . .

Now, Master, you may let your servant go in peace, according to your word. *Lk 2:29*
Hail Mary . . .

For my eyes have seen your salvation, which you prepared in sight of all the peoples, a light for

revelation to the Gentiles, and glory for your people Israel. *Lk 2:30-32*
Hail Mary . . .

I will make you a light to the nations, / that my salvation may reach to the ends of the earth. *Is 49:6*
Hail Mary . . .

For a child is born to us, a son is given us; / upon his shoulder dominion rests. / They name him Wonder-Counselor, God-Hero, / Father-Forever, Prince of Peace. *Is 9:5*
Hail Mary . . .

A shoot shall sprout from the stump of Jesse . . . Justice shall be the band around his waist, / and faithfulness a belt upon his hips. *Is 11:1, 5*
Hail Mary . . .

He has sent me to bring glad tidings to the lowly . . . To proclaim liberty to the captives / and release to the prisoners. *Is 61:1*
Hail Mary . . .

Here is my servant whom I uphold, / my chosen one with whom I am pleased, / Upon whom I have put my spirit; / he shall bring forth justice to the nations. *Is 42:1*
Hail Mary . . .
Glory be . . .

LORD JESUS, LEAD US IN FORTITUDE AS WE WORK FOR THE FULFILLMENT OF GOD'S KINGDOM.

Fifth Joyful Mystery
THE FINDING OF JESUS

Mary and Joseph find Jesus in the temple when he is lost for three days during Passover.
Our Father . . .

They journeyed for a day and looked for him among their relatives and acquaintances, but not finding him, they returned to Jerusalem to look for him. After three days they found him in the temple. *Lk 2:44-46*
Hail Mary . . .

Sitting in the midst of the teachers, listening to them and asking them questions, and all who heard him were astounded at his understanding and his answers. *Lk 2:46-47*
Hail Mary . . .

When his parents saw him, they were astonished, and his mother said to him, "Son, why have you done this to us?" *Lk 2:48*
Hail Mary . . .

And he said to them, "Why were you looking for me?" *Lk 2:49*
Hail Mary . . .

First Luminous Mystery
BAPTISM IN THE JORDAN

Jesus begins his public ministry being baptized by John.
Our Father . . .

For our sake he made him to be sin who did not know sin, so that we might become the righteousness of God in him. *2 Cor 5:21*
Hail Mary . . .

He went throughout (the) whole region of the Jordan, proclaiming a baptism of repentance for the forgiveness of sins, as it is written in . . . Isaiah: "A voice of one crying out in the desert: 'Prepare the way of the Lord, make straight his paths.'" *Lk 3:3*
Hail Mary . . .

And the crowds asked him, "What then should we do?" He said to them in reply, "Whoever has two cloaks should share with the person who has none. And whoever has food should do likewise." *Lk 3:10-11*
Hail Mary . . .

Jesus also had been baptized . . . heaven was opened and the holy Spirit descended upon him in bodily form like a dove. And a voice came from heaven, "You are my beloved Son; with you I am well pleased." *Lk 3:21-22*
Hail Mary . . .

Did you not know that I must be in my Father's house? *Lk 2:49*
Hail Mary . . .

While he was still speaking to the crowds, his mother and his brothers appeared outside, wishing to speak with him. *Mt 12:46*
Hail Mary . . .

Someone told him, "Your mother and your brothers are standing outside, asking to speak with you."
Mt 12:47
Hail Mary . . .

But he said in reply to the one who told him, "Who is my mother? Who are my brothers?" *Mt 12:48*
Hail Mary . . .

"For whoever does the will of my heavenly Father is my brother, and sister, and mother." *Mt 12:50*
Hail Mary . . .

"Amen, I say to you, whatever you did for one of these least brothers of mine, you did for me."
Mt 25:40
Hail Mary . . .
Glory be . . .

LORD JESUS, LET OUR LIVES BEAR WITNESS
TO GOD'S LOVE FOR US.

Here is my servant whom I uphold, / my chosen one with whom I am pleased, / Upon whom I have put my spirit. *Is 42:1*
Hail Mary . . .

A bruised reed he shall not break, / and a smoldering wick he shall not quench. *Is 42:3*
Hail Mary . . .

I, the LORD, have called you for the victory of justice. *Is 42:6*
Hail Mary . . .

I formed you, and set you / as a covenant of the people, / a light for the nations. *Is 42:6*
Hail Mary . . .

"The Spirit of the Lord is upon me, / because he has anointed me / to bring glad tidings to the poor." *Lk 4:18*
Hail Mary . . .

"He has sent me to proclaim liberty to captives / and recovery of sight to the blind, / to let the oppressed go free, / and to proclaim a year acceptable to the Lord." *Lk 4:18-19*
Hail Mary . . .
Glory be . . .

LORD JESUS, HELP US TO PERSEVERE IN
LIVING OUT OUR BAPTISMAL PROMISES.

Second Luminous Mystery
THE WEDDING AT CANA

Jesus performs his first public sign revealing his true identity, at the request of his mother.
Our Father . . .

When the wine ran short, the mother of Jesus said to him, "They have no wine." *Jn 2:3*
Hail Mary . . .

Jesus said to her, "Woman, how does your concern affect me? My hour has not yet come." *Jn 2:4*
Hail Mary . . .

His mother said to the servers, "Do whatever he tells you." *Jn 2:5*
Hail Mary . . .

Jesus told them, "Fill the jars with water." So they filled them to the brim. Then he told them, "Draw some out now and take it to the headwaiter." *Jn 2:7-8*
Hail Mary . . .

The headwaiter called the bridegroom and said to him, "Everyone serves good wine first, and then when people have drunk freely, an inferior one; but you have kept the good wine until now." *Jn 2:9-10*
Hail Mary . . .

If I . . . have washed your feet, you ought to wash one another's feet. I have given you a model to follow, so that as I have done for you, you should also do.
Jn 13:14-15
Hail Mary . . .

To you who hear I say, love your enemies, do good to those who hate you, bless those who curse you, pray for those who mistreat you. *Lk 6:27-28*
Hail Mary . . .

Stop judging and you will not be judged. Stop condemning and you will not be condemned. Forgive and you will be forgiven. *Lk 6:37*
Hail Mary . . .

Then he said to all, "If anyone wishes to come after me, he must deny himself and take up his cross daily and follow me." *Lk 9:23*
Hail Mary . . .

This is my commandment: love one another as I love you. *Jn 15:12*
Hail Mary . . .
Glory be . . .

LORD JESUS, OPEN US TO THE POWER OF YOUR
GRACE TO CHANGE OUR HEARTS AND LIVES.

Third Luminous Mystery
PROCLAMATION OF THE KINGDOM OF GOD

After John was arrested, Jesus began proclaiming the Good News of God's kingdom.
Our Father . . .

Jesus came to Galilee proclaiming the gospel of God.
Mk 1:14
Hail Mary . . .

This is the time of fulfillment. The kingdom of God is at hand. Repent, and believe in the gospel. *Mk 1:15*
Hail Mary . . .

The Spirit of the Lord is upon me, / because he has anointed me / to bring glad tidings to the poor.
Lk 4:18
Hail Mary . . .

He has sent me to proclaim liberty to captives / and recovery of sight to the blind, / to let the oppressed go free, / and to proclaim a year acceptable to the Lord.
Lk 4:18-19
Hail Mary . . .

Today this scripture passage is fulfilled in your hearing. *Lk 4:21*
Hail Mary . . .

You have heard that it was said, "An eye for an eye and a tooth for a tooth." But I say to you . . . when someone strikes you on [your] right cheek, turn the other one to him as well. *Mt 5:38-39*
Hail Mary . . .

You have heard that it was said, "You shall love your neighbor and hate your enemy." But I say to you, love your enemies, and pray for those who persecute you. *Mt 5:43-44*
Hail Mary . . .

Do not store up for yourselves treasures on earth . . . But store up treasures in heaven . . . for where your treasure is, there also will your heart be. *Mt 6:19-21*
Hail Mary . . .

Do to others whatever you would have them do to you. This is the law and the prophets. *Mt 7:12*
Hail Mary . . .

Without cost you have received; without cost you are to give. *Mt 10:8*
Hail Mary . . .
Glory be . . .

LORD JESUS, FILL US WITH THE DESIRE TO
STRIVE FOR ONGOING CONVERSION.

Fourth Luminous Mystery
THE TRANSFIGURATION

Jesus is seen with Moses and Elijah, confirming that his suffering will end in glory.
Our Father . . .

Jesus took Peter, James, and John his brother, and led them up a high mountain by themselves. And he was transfigured before them; his face shone like the sun and his clothes became white as light. *Mt 17:1-2*
Hail Mary . . .

Two men were conversing with him, Moses and Elijah, who appeared in glory and spoke of his exodus that he was going to accomplish in Jerusalem. *Lk 9:30-31*
Hail Mary . . .

Peter and his companions . . . saw his glory and the two men standing with him. *Lk 9:32*
Hail Mary . . .

Peter said . . . "Master, it is good that we are here; let us make three tents. . . ." But he did not know what he was saying. *Lk 9:33*
Hail Mary . . .

A voice [said], "This is my beloved Son, with whom I am well pleased; listen to him." *Mt 17:5*
Hail Mary . . .

But Jesus came and touched them, saying, "Rise, and do not be afraid." And when the disciples raised their eyes, they saw no one else but Jesus alone. *Mt 17:7-8*
Hail Mary . . .

Through him was life, and this life was the light of the human race; the light shines in the darkness, and the darkness has not overcome it. *Jn 1:4-5*
Hail Mary . . .

No one has ever seen God. The only Son, God, who is at the Father's side, has revealed him. *Jn 1:18*
Hail Mary . . .

All of us, gazing with unveiled face on the glory of the Lord, are being transformed into the same image from glory to glory, as from the Lord who is the Spirit.
2 Cor 3:18
Hail Mary . . .

You are the light of the world . . . your light must shine before others, that they may see your good deeds and glorify your heavenly Father. *Mt 5:14, 16*
Hail Mary . . .
Glory be . . .

LORD JESUS, GRANT US THE COURAGE TO
SHINE YOUR LIGHT IN OUR LIVES.

Fifth Luminous Mystery
INSTITUTION OF THE EUCHARIST

At the last supper, Jesus instructs us to remember him in celebration of the Eucharist.
Our Father . . .

Before the feast of Passover, Jesus knew that his hour had come to pass from this world to the Father. He loved his own in the world and he loved them to the end. *Jn 13:1*
Hail Mary . . .

My appointed time draws near; in your house I shall celebrate the Passover with my disciples. *Mt 26:18*
Hail Mary . . .

I have eagerly desired to eat this Passover with you before I suffer, for, I tell you, I shall not eat it [again] until there is fulfillment in the kingdom of God.
Lk 22:15-16
Hail Mary . . .

Then he took the bread, said the blessing, broke it, and gave it to them, saying, "This is my body, which will be given for you; do this in memory of me."
Lk 22:19
Hail Mary . . .

And likewise the cup after they had eaten, saying,
"This cup is the new covenant in my blood, which will
be shed for you." *Lk 22:20*
Hail Mary . . .

For as often as you eat this bread and drink the cup,
you proclaim the death of the Lord until he comes.
1 Cor 11:26
Hail Mary . . .

I pray not only for them, but also for those who will
believe in me through their word, so that they may all
be one . . . that the world may believe that you sent
me. *Jn 17:20-21*
Hail Mary . . .

Now you are Christ's body, and individually parts of
it. *1 Cor 12:27*
Hail Mary . . .

For in one Spirit we were all baptized into one body,
whether Jews or Greeks, slaves or free persons, and we
were all given to drink of one Spirit. *1 Cor 12:13*
Hail Mary . . .

If [one] part suffers, all the parts suffer with it; if one
part is honored, all the parts share its joy. *1 Cor 12:26*
Hail Mary . . .
Glory be . . .

LORD JESUS, MAKE OF US A SIGN OF THE
UNITY FOR WHICH YOU PRAYED.

First Sorrowful Mystery
AGONY IN THE GARDEN

After the Last Supper, Jesus takes his friends to pray in the Garden of Gethsemane.
Our Father . . .

Then he said to them, "My soul is sorrowful even to death. Remain here and keep watch." *Mk 14:34*
Hail Mary . . .

Abba, Father, all things are possible to you. Take this cup away from me, but not what I will but what you will. *Mk 14:36*
Hail Mary . . .

He was in such agony and he prayed so fervently that his sweat became like drops of blood falling on the ground. *Lk 22:44*
Hail Mary . . .

Then he returned once more and found them asleep, for they could not keep their eyes open and did not know what to answer him. *Mk 14:40*
Hail Mary . . .

Get up, let us go. Look, my betrayer is at hand. *Mt 26:46*
Hail Mary . . .

At that hour Jesus said to the crowds, "Have you come out as against a robber, with swords and clubs to seize me?" *Mt 26:55*
Hail Mary . . .

And behold, one of those who accompanied Jesus put his hand to his sword, drew it, and struck the high priest's servant, cutting off his ear. *Mt 26:51*
Hail Mary . . .

Jesus said to him, "Put your sword back into its sheath, for all who take the sword will perish by the sword." *Mt 26:52*
Hail Mary . . .

They shall beat their swords into plowshares / and their spears into pruning hooks. *Is 2:4*
Hail Mary . . .

One nation shall not raise the sword against another, nor shall they train for war again. *Is 2:4*
Hail Mary . . .
Glory be . . .

LORD JESUS, STRENGTHEN OUR TRUST
IN GOD'S LOVING PRESENCE.

Second Sorrowful Mystery
SCOURGING AT THE PILLAR

Pontius Pilate has Jesus whipped by Roman soldiers.
Our Father . . .

The high priest questioned Jesus about his disciples
and about his doctrine. *Jn 18:19*
Hail Mary . . .

Why ask me? Ask those who heard me what I said to
them. They know what I said. *Jn 18:21*
Hail Mary . . .

The chief priests and the entire Sanhedrin kept trying
to obtain testimony against Jesus in order to put him
to death, but they found none. *Mk 14:55*
Hail Mary . . .

The whole Sanhedrin held a council. They bound
Jesus, led him away, and handed him over to Pilate.
Mk 15:1
Hail Mary . . .

Then Pilate took Jesus and had him scourged. *Jn 19:1*
Hail Mary . . .

After he had Jesus scourged, he handed him over to be
crucified. *Mt 27:26*
Hail Mary . . .

Go and tell John what you have seen and heard: the blind regain their sight, the lame walk. *Lk 7:22*
Hail Mary . . .

Lepers are cleansed, the deaf hear. *Lk 7:22*
Hail Mary . . .

The dead are raised, the poor have the good news proclaimed to them. *Lk 7:22*
Hail Mary . . .

You say I am a king. For this I was born and for this I came into the world, to testify to the truth. Everyone who belongs to the truth listens to my voice. *Jn 18:37*
Hail Mary . . .
Glory be . . .

LORD JESUS, EMBOLDEN US TO SPEAK THE TRUTH
EVEN IN THE FACE OF RESISTANCE.

Third Sorrowful Mystery
THORNS

Soldiers strip and mock Jesus and crown him with thorns.
Our Father . . .

They stripped off his clothes. *Mt 27:28*
Hail Mary . . .

Weaving a crown out of thorns, they placed it on his head, and a reed in his right hand. And kneeling before him, they mocked him, saying, "Hail, King of the Jews!" *Mt 27:29*
Hail Mary . . .

They spat upon him and took the reed and kept striking him on the head. *Mt 27:30*
Hail Mary . . .

When they had mocked him, they stripped him of the cloak, dressed him in his own clothes, and led him off to crucify him. *Mt 27:31*
Hail Mary . . .

Pilate said to them, "Shall I crucify your king?" The chief priests answered, "We have no king but Caesar." *Jn 19:15*
Hail Mary . . .

Through his suffering, my servant shall justify many.
Is 53:11
Hail Mary . . .

Oppressed and condemned, he was taken away.
Is 53:8
Hail Mary . . .

I gave my back to those who beat me, / my cheeks to those who plucked my beard; / My face I did not shield from buffets and spitting. *Is 50:6*
Hail Mary . . .

Hear me, you who know justice, / you people who have my teaching at heart. *Is 51:7*
Hail Mary . . .

How beautiful upon the mountains / are the feet of him who brings glad tidings, / Announcing peace, bearing good news, / announcing salvation, and saying to Zion, / "Your God is King!" *Is 52:7*
Hail Mary . . .
Glory be . . .

LORD JESUS, LET US FOLLOW YOUR EXAMPLE OF
FAITHFULNESS IN TIMES OF SUFFERING.

Fourth Sorrowful Mystery
JESUS CARRIES THE CROSS

Jesus travels the Way of the Cross.
Our Father . . .

So they took Jesus, and carrying the cross himself he went out to what is called the Place of the Skull, in Hebrew, Golgotha. *Jn 19:16-17*
Hail Mary . . .

A large crowd of people followed Jesus, including many women who mourned and lamented him.
Lk 23:27
Hail Mary . . .

As they were going out, they met a Cyrenian named Simon; this man they pressed into service to carry his cross. *Mt 27:32*
Hail Mary . . .

They gave him wine drugged with myrrh, but he did not take it. *Mk 15:23*
Hail Mary . . .

After they had crucified him, they divided his garments by casting lots. *Mt 27:35*
Hail Mary . . .

Jesus said, "Father, forgive them, they know not what they do." *Lk 23:34*
Hail Mary . . .

He said to them, "This is my blood of the covenant, which will be shed for many."
Mk 14:24
Hail Mary . . .

"I shall not drink again the fruit of the vine until the day when I drink it new in the kingdom of God."
Mk 14:25
Hail Mary . . .

Then Jesus said to his disciples, "Whoever wishes to come after me must deny himself, take up his cross, and follow me." *Mt 16:24*
Hail Mary . . .

For whoever wishes to save his life will lose it, but whoever loses his life for my sake will find it.
Mt 16:25
Hail Mary . . .
Glory be . . .

LORD JESUS, STRENGTHEN US AS WE WALK IN YOUR FOOTSTEPS TO LIVE TRUE FORGIVENESS.

Fifth Sorrowful Mystery
THE CRUCIFIXION

Jesus dies on the cross.
Our Father . . .

When they came to the place called the Skull, they crucified him and the criminals there, one on his right, the other on his left. *Lk 23:33*
Hail Mary . . .

And they placed over his head the written charge against him: This is Jesus, the King of the Jews.
Mt 27:37
Hail Mary . . .

Those passing by reviled him, shaking their heads.
Mt 27:39
Hail Mary . . .

The revolutionaries who were crucified with him also kept abusing him in the same way. *Mt 27:44*
Hail Mary . . .

Jesus gave a loud cry and breathed his last. *Mk 15:37*
Hail Mary . . .

All who see me mock me; / they curl their lips and jeer; / they shake their heads at me. *Ps 22:8*
Hail Mary . . .

So wasted are my hands and feet / that I can count all
my bones. *Ps 22:17-18*
Hail Mary . . .

They divide my garments among them; / for my
clothing they cast lots. *Ps 22:19*
Hail Mary . . .

But you, LORD, do not stay far off; / my strength,
come quickly to help me. *Ps 22:20*
Hail Mary . . .

The generation to come will be told of the Lord,
that they may proclaim to a people yet unborn
the deliverance you have brought. *Ps 22:32*
Hail Mary . . .
Glory be . . .

LORD JESUS, HEAL THE BROKENNESS OF YOUR PEOPLE.
MAY WE BEAR WITNESS TO YOUR LOVE BY GROWING
IN UNITY WITH ONE ANOTHER.

First Glorious Mystery
THE RESURRECTION

Jesus rises to new life.
Our Father . . .

But at daybreak on the first day of the week they took
the spices they had prepared and went to the tomb.
Lk 24:1
Hail Mary . . .

They found the stone rolled away from the tomb; but
when they entered, they did not find the body of the
Lord Jesus. *Lk 24:2-3*
Hail Mary . . .

Why do you seek the living one among the dead? He is
not here, but he has been raised. *Lk 24:5-6*
Hail Mary . . .

Then they went away quickly from the tomb, fearful
yet overjoyed, and ran to announce this to his disciples.
Mt 28:8
Hail Mary . . .

Jesus met them on their way and greeted them. They
approached, embraced his feet, and did him homage.
Mt 28:9
Hail Mary . . .

I am the resurrection and the life. *Jn 11:25*
Hail Mary . . .

Everyone who lives and believes in me will never die.
Jn 11:26
Hail Mary . . .

I have told you this so that you might have peace in
me. *Jn 16:33*
Hail Mary . . .

In the world you will have trouble, but take courage.
Jn 16:33
Hail Mary . . .

I have conquered the world. *Jn 16:33*
Hail Mary . . .
Glory be . . .

LORD JESUS, RENEW OUR BELIEF IN GOD'S
PROMISE OF FAITHFULNESS.

Second Glorious Mystery
THE ASCENSION

Jesus ascends into heaven after instructing his disciples.
Our Father . . .

Then he led them [out] as far as Bethany, raised his hands, and blessed them. As he blessed them he parted from them and was taken up to heaven. *Lk 24:50-51*
Hail Mary . . .

All power in heaven and on earth has been given to me. *Mt 28:18*
Hail Mary . . .

Go, therefore, and make disciples of all nations. *Mt 28:19*
Hail Mary . . .

I am with you always, until the end of the age. *Mt 28:20*
Hail Mary . . .

So then the Lord Jesus, after he spoke to them, was taken up into heaven and took his seat at the right hand of God. *Mk 16:19*
Hail Mary . . .

See, my servant shall prosper, / he shall be raised high and greatly exalted. *Is 52:13*
Hail Mary . . .

So shall he startle many nations, / because of him kings shall stand speechless. *Is 52:15*
Hail Mary . . .

He shall see his descendants in a long life, / and the will of the LORD shall be accomplished through him. *Is 53:10*
Hail Mary . . .

Because of his affliction / he shall see the light in fullness of days. *Is 53:11*
Hail Mary . . .

He shall take away the sins of many, / and win pardon for their offenses. *Is 53:12*
Hail Mary . . .
Glory be . . .

LORD JESUS, INSTILL IN US GENUINE HOPE OF HEAVEN
AS WE CONTINUE TO BEAR WITNESS TO YOUR
PRESENCE THROUGH OUR WORK HERE
ON EARTH.

Third Glorious Mystery
THE DESCENT OF THE HOLY SPIRIT

The Holy Spirit fills the disciples of Jesus on Pentecost.
Our Father . . .

And suddenly there came from the sky a noise like a strong driving wind, and it filled the entire house in which they were. *Acts 2:2*
Hail Mary . . .

Then there appeared to them tongues as of fire, which parted and came to rest on each one of them. *Acts 2:3*
Hail Mary . . .

And they were all filled with the holy Spirit. *Acts 2:4*
Hail Mary . . .

And began to speak in different tongues, as the Spirit enabled them to proclaim. *Acts 2:4*
Hail Mary . . .

The Spirit of the Lord is upon me, / because he has anointed me. *Lk 4:18*
Hail Mary . . .

To bring glad tidings to the poor. / He has sent me to proclaim liberty to captives. *Lk 4:18*
Hail Mary . . .

Recovery of sight to
the blind, / to let the
oppressed
go free. *Lk 4:18*
Hail Mary . . .

Whoever believes in
me will do the works
that I do, and will
do greater ones than
these. *Jn 14:12*
Hail Mary . . .

The Advocate, the
holy Spirit that the
Father will send in
my name—he will
teach you everything
and remind you
of all that [I] told
you. *Jn 14:26*
Hail Mary . . .

Awe came upon
everyone, and many wonders and signs were done
through the apostles. All who believed were together
and had all things in common. *Acts 2:43-44*
Hail Mary . . .
Glory be . . .

LORD JESUS, FILL US WITH YOUR SPIRIT
AND TRUE ZEAL FOR JUSTICE.

Fourth Glorious Mystery
THE ASSUMPTION

Mary is taken body and soul into heaven.
Our Father . . .

Blessed are you, daughter, by the Most High God,
above all the women on earth. *Jdt 13:18*
Hail Mary . . .

Your deed of hope will never be forgotten by those
who tell of the might of God. *Jdt 13:19*
Hail Mary . . .

You risked your life when your people were being
oppressed. *Jdt 13:20*
Hail Mary . . .

You are the glory of Jerusalem, the surpassing joy of
Israel; You are the splendid boast of our people.
Jdt 15:9
Hail Mary . . .

God is pleased with what you have wrought. May you
be blessed by the Lord Almighty forever and ever!
Jdt 15:10
Hail Mary . . .

All glorious is the king's daughter as she enters, / her
raiment threaded with gold. *Ps 45:14*
Hail Mary . . .

In embroidered apparel she is led to the king. *Ps 45:15*
Hail Mary . . .

I will make your name renowned through all genera-
tions; / thus nations shall praise you forever. *Ps 45:18*
Hail Mary . . .

Then God's temple in heaven was opened, and the ark
of his covenant could be seen in the temple. *Rev 11:19*
Hail Mary . . .

A great sign appeared in the sky, a woman clothed
with the sun, with the moon under her feet, and on
her head a crown of twelve stars. *Rev 12:1*
Hail Mary . . .
Glory be . . .

LORD JESUS, INSPIRE US WITH GRATITUDE
FOR ALL GOD'S GIFTS.

Fifth Glorious Mystery
THE CORONATION OF MARY

Mary takes her place in the heavenly reign of God.
Our Father . . .

In the assembly of the Most High she opens her mouth, in the presence of his hosts she declares her worth. *Sir 24:2*
Hail Mary . . .

Come to me, all you that yearn for me, / and be filled with my fruits. *Sir 24:18*
Hail Mary . . .

In the holy tent I ministered before him. *Sir 24:10*
Hail Mary . . .

Thus in the chosen city he has given me rest. *Sir 24:11*
Hail Mary . . .

In the highest heavens did I dwell, / my throne on a pillar of cloud. *Sir 24:4*
Hail Mary . . .

For I was hungry and you gave me food. *Mt 25:35*
Hail Mary . . .

I was thirsty and you gave me drink. *Mt 25:35*
Hail Mary . . .

A stranger and you welcomed me, naked and you
clothed me. *Mt 25:35-36*
Hail Mary . . .

Ill and you cared for me, in prison and you visited me.
Mt 25:36
Hail Mary . . .

"Amen, I say to you, whatever you did for one of
these least brothers of mine, you did for me."
Mt 25:40
Hail Mary . . .
Glory be . . .

LORD JESUS, MAY WE LIVE LIVES OF CONTINUOUS
PRAISE AND THANKSGIVING, JOYFULLY
FOLLOWING YOUR WAY.